Science Toys & Tricks

Laurence B. White, Jr.

drawings by
Marc Tolon Brown

 HarperTrophy
A Division of HarperCollinsPublishers

To Dave. . .
who guarantees every experiment
because they worked for him

First published by Addison-Wesley Publishing Company
Science Toys & Tricks
Science Toys: text copyright © 1975 by Laurence B. White, Jr.
Illustrations copyright © 1975 by Marc Tolon Brown
Science Tricks: text copyright © 1975 by Laurence B. White, Jr.
Illustrations copyright © 1975 by Marc Tolon Brown

Library of Congress Cataloging in Publication Data
White, Laurence B.
  Science toys & tricks.

  Reprint. Originally published. Reading, Mass.:
Addison-Wesley, © 1975.
  Summary: Directions for simple science tricks
experiments, and projects that demonstrate basic
scientific principles.
  1. Science—Experiments—Juvenile literature.
2. Scientific recreations—Juvenile literature.
[1. Science—Experiments. 2. Scientific recreations.
3. Experiments] I. Brown, Marc Tolon, ill. II. Title.
III. Title: Science toys and tricks.
Q164.W48 1985b   507'8   84-40787
ISBN 0-201-08659-X

  (A Harper Trophy Book)
ISBN 0-06-446014-2 (pbk.)   85-43036

First Harper Trophy edition, 1985.

Toys are to Make

Toys are made to play with.
So are these things toys?

- a paper flower that blooms in a glass of water.
- A ghost that sticks to the wall when you rub it.
- A balloon dog that rolls on his back
  at your command.

They are all toys, but they are a special kind.
Science makes them work.
It makes the flower bloom, the ghost stick,
and the dog roll.
You'll find here lots of toys like these.
You need just a little science to start toys
working for you.

A Flower That Blooms

Cut a flower out of a paper towel.

Make it about this big.

Fold the petals down.

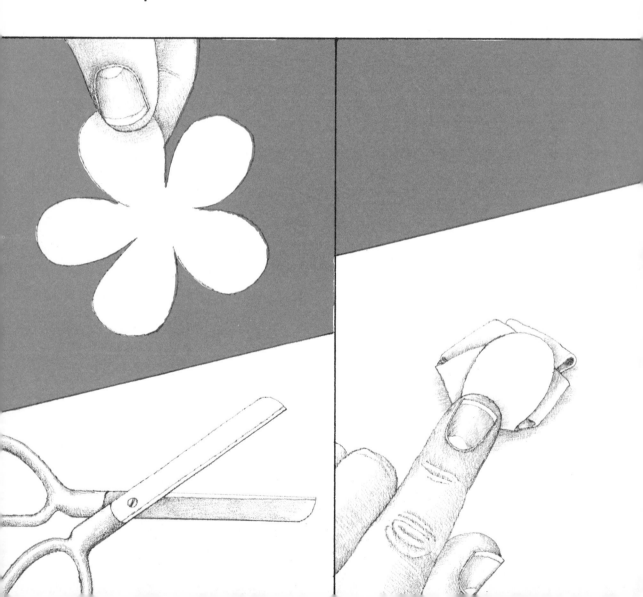

Drop the folded flower into a glass of water.

The paper soaks up some water.

The water makes the paper swell up.

Quickly . . . the petals open.

And the flower blooms.

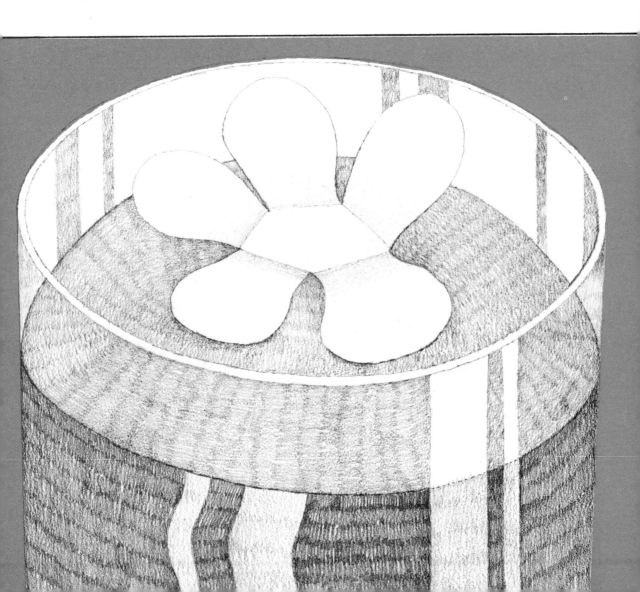

A Magic Card

Take a piece of cardboard.
Draw some straight lines across it.
Make the lines dark.
Push a pencil through the middle.
Spin the card on the pencil.
Look!
The straight lines change to curved lines.
The card is not really magic.
Straight lines just look curved,
because they are going around.

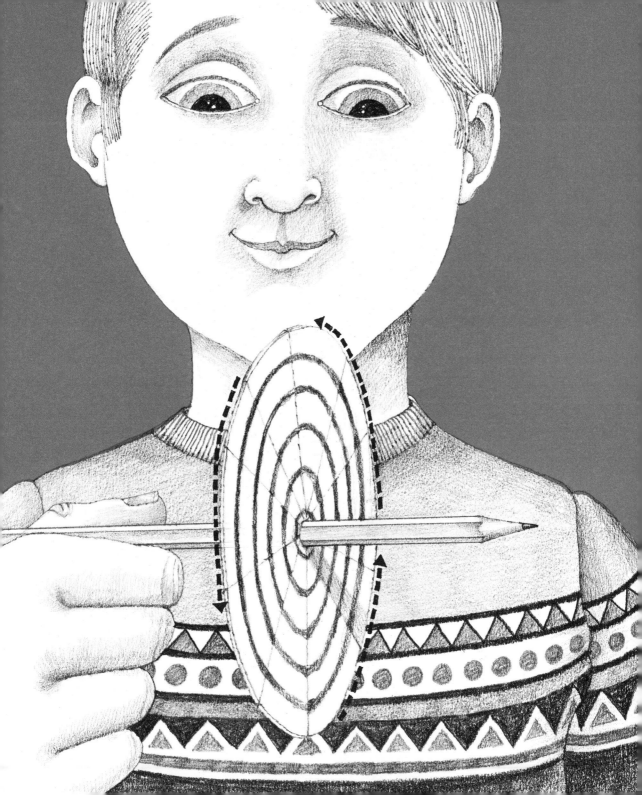

A Man That Moves

Fold a long strip of paper in half.

Draw a man on the bottom.

Draw another man on top.

Make their arms and legs different.

Hold the top sheet by one corner.

Flick it up and down quickly.

You will see the man move.

He seems to move his arms and legs.

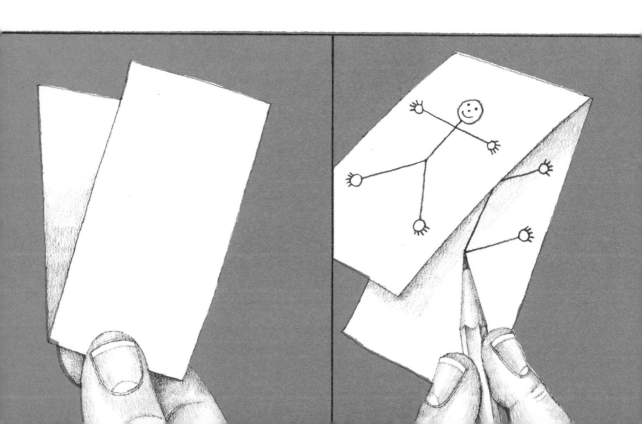

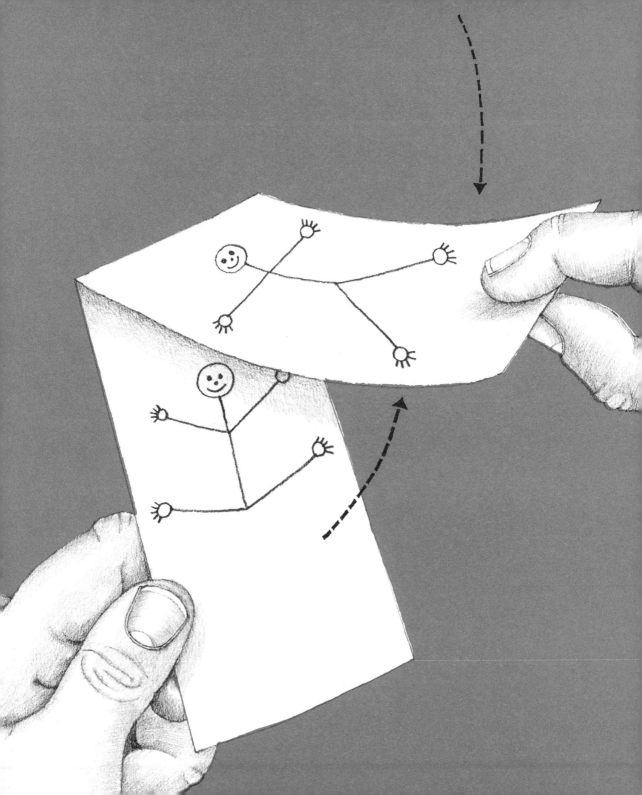

Fold a Fan

Fold a big piece of paper.
Fold it back and forth,
and back and forth again and again.
Hold it by one end.
Open the other end out.
Fan your face.
You cannot see air.
Or touch it or taste it.
But you feel it when it moves.
On a hot day fanning your face certainly feels good.

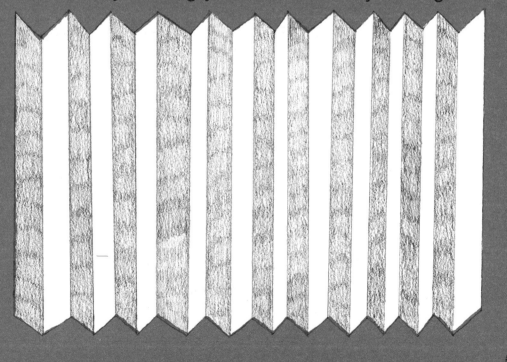

Fold a Spooky Screamer

Cut a piece of paper about this big.
Fold it in three places.

Hold it between your fingers.
Put your lips right against it.
Blow hard in the middle.
Blowing air can make spooky sounds.
Your breath is a little wind.
It will make the paper scream!

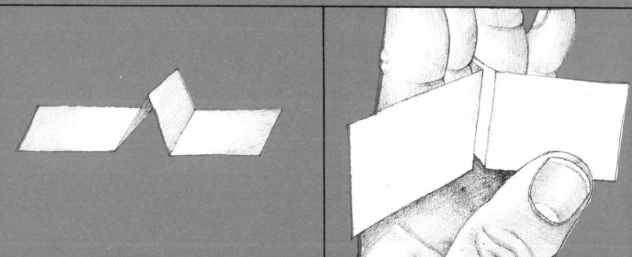

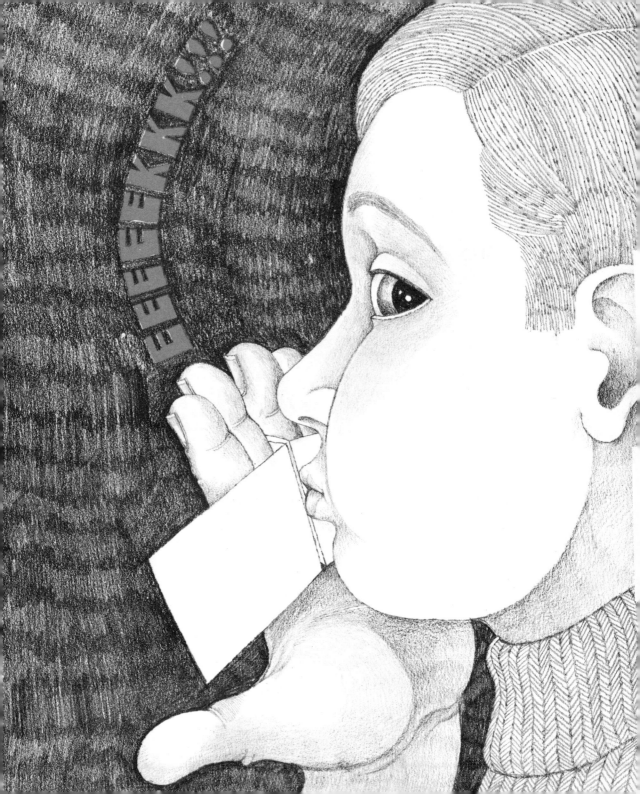

Fly an Air Spinner

Cut a long strip of paper.
Fold the two flaps down.
One one way, one the other way.
Put a paper clip on the bottom.
Drop the folded paper.
The air pushes on it.
Air makes it move.
It spins as it floats down.

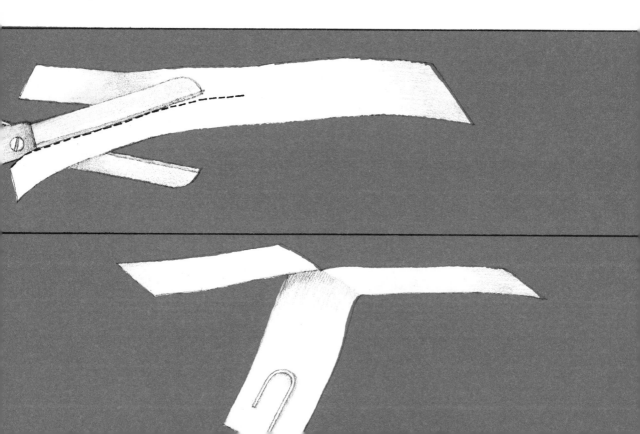

A Strange Airplane

Cut two strips of heavy paper.

Tape them in loops.

Tape the loops to a drinking straw.

Toss it in the air.

It flies!

It has no wings or tail,

but the air holds it up.

Airplanes can be different shapes.

A Water Magnifying Glass

Cut a big hole in a piece of cardboard.
Cover it with clear plastic food wrap.
Lay it on a picture in a newspaper.
Let one drop of water fall on the plastic.
Look at the picture through the drop.
You will see lots of dots.
Newspaper pictures are made of dots.
Lift the water magnifying glass a little.
The dots look even bigger.

mex Prices Drop...

By JAMES J. NAGLE

rices continued their down-
slide yesterday on the
erican Stock Exchange as
banks increased their
me lending rate to 10 per
nt. Prices closed mixed in
e over-the-counter market.
The Amex market value in-
ex finished at 94.01, down .25
ith declines outnumbering ad-
ances 336 to 247, while 327
ssues were unchanged. The
price of an average share lost
3 cents as volume declined
slightly to 1,652,000 shares
compared with 1,659,000 shares
the day before. There were nine
large blocks against two on
Wednesday.

In the counter market,
the NASDAQ industrial index
rose .04 to 84.07, while the
composite index was off .08 to
89.79. There were 444 declines
compared with 334 advances,
while 1,939 issues were unchanged. Sales dropped to 3.
827,000 shares, compared with
4.57 million shares the day before.

On the Amex the most active
issue was Syntex, which gained
2¼ to 47⅞ on 81,800 shares.
Champion Home Builders
slipped ⅛ to 4⅞ on the trading
of 66,600 shares, including a
block of 52,800 at 4⅞. Execu-
tone Inc., tumbled 1⅛ to 6⅞
on a turnover of 48,700 shares,
including a block of 38,900 at
6⅛.

The most active issue in the

counter market, was Pan American Bankshare, off 1 to 11½.
Pabst Brew-
ing Company was up ¾ to 16⅜
on 127,100 shares. Ring Around
Productions dropped ⅛ to 8⅝
on 76,200 shares. American Ex-
press was unchanged at 41¼
on 47,400 shares, Agnico Eagle
Mines was off ¼ to 8⅞ on
44,900 shares.

Missouri Beef Packers slipped
⅜ to 14½ on the Amex. The
beef processor said it would
suspend slaughtering operations
at its Boise, Idaho, facility today because current prices of
live cattle in the Northwest
"do not permit it to operate."
It said other operations at the
plant will continue.

Real estate investment trusts
were lower as analysts at-
tributed recent losses to indus-
try problems, including tight
money and a housing slump.
American Fletcher Mortgage
slipped ¼ to 19½. Beneficial

Standard Mortgage Investors
lost ½ to 16¼. Hotel Investors
dropped ⅜ to 10⅝ and Heit-
man Mortgage Investors dipped
¼ to 9¼.

Among the movers on the
Amex, Fidelco Growth Investors added 1¼ to 16¾. NUMAC
Oil and Gas lost 1 to 15⅞.
Recrion declined 1⅜ to 34⅜.
Pittsburgh-Des Moines Steel fell
1⅛ to 28½ and Houston Oil
and Minerals advanced 1¾ to
46.

Medical equipment and facili-
ties issues were narrowly
higher. Den-Tal-Ez rose ¼ to
5⅝. Community Psychiatric
Centers added ¼ to 7⅜. Med-
enco, Inc., tacked on ⅛ to 6¼.
Hilhaven, Inc., edged up ⅛ to
3¾ and Huntington Health
Service, Inc., added ½ to 2⅛.

Percentage Gains

Stocks with the largest percentage gains on the American
Stock Exchange yesterday.

Stock	Last Price	Net Chge.
Plaza Grp	4	+1
Sec Mfg Inv	4⅜	+⅜
Seaport Cp	4½	+⅜
Goodrich wf	1	+⅛
Fsl Denv wf	1¼	+1½

Percentage Drops

Stocks with the largest percentage drops on the American
Stock Exchange yesterday.

Stock	Last Price	Net Chge.	Pct.
Bk vl Wt wf	1	—	-20.0
AmStr	⅞		-20.0
ARA	4⅝		-20.0
AricP	8⅝	8.5	-16.7
Armst	4⅝	4.3	

become
at the
anks, also

quoted at
evel in the
Reserve
o carry out
agreements.

xpected

plying trans-
Good Friday
weekend, ap-
le immediate
d's rate that
d the close of
3/16 per cent
range.

for this week
articipants in
nd tax-exempt
ly concentrated
corporate obliga-
positions" for
long weekend.
ng and trading
be open today,

atching up posi-
day, corporate
ome modest price
tly marketed util-
corporate obliga-
004, for example,
a point on the day
estern Bell's 8⅛s,
were marked down
nt.

xempt Market

exempt market on
hand showed some
headway from
y's upturn. The
00 Florida State
Education offering of
obligation bonds,
expected to b
sterday, is now
calendar. Sch
April 16.
measures of
market's p
were repo
the Bond Bu
yields on 2
pal bonds fo
yesterday
asis (one o
percentage
the level fo
week. This
ugh a conti
steady up

Electric Ghost

Cut a spooky ghost out of newspaper.

Color it any way you like.

Put it flat on your wall.

Rub it hard with the side of a wood pencil.

Rub it back and forth, all over.

Take the pencil away.

Your spooky ghost sticks by itself.

Static electricity makes the paper stick.

Rubbing makes static electricity.

This Cup Hums

Cut the bottom out of a paper cup.

Cover the top with wax paper.

Hold it on with a rubber band.

Touch your lips to the wax paper.

Sing or hum into it.

Your humming makes the air move.

The air makes the wax paper move.

The cup hums along with you.

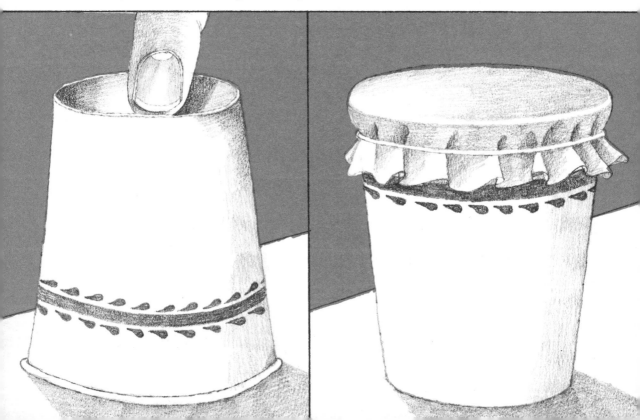

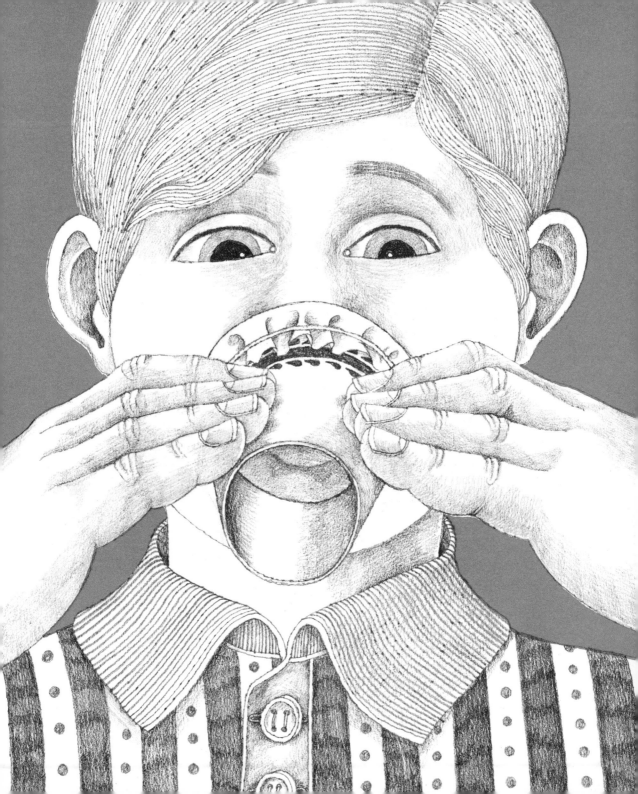

The Cup That Roars

Tie a paper clip on a piece of string.

Make a tiny hole in the bottom of a paper cup.

Poke the string through the hole.

Rub your thumbnail down the string,

while you are squeezing the string tightly.

You'll hear a "ROAR!".

The box is like a drum.

It makes the sound of your rubbing loud.

Try rubbing the string without the cup.

What happens?

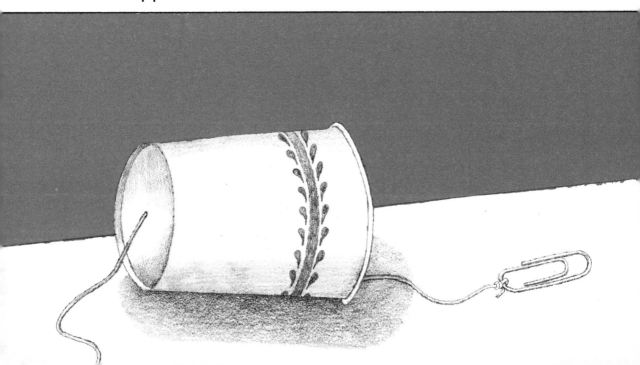

Three Note Music Maker

Put a rubber band around a book.
Slip a paper cup under the band.
Move the cup toward one end.
Snap the band.
It makes a musical note.
Snap it in another place.
The rubber band is like a guitar string.
Your music maker can make three different notes.
Keep snapping in different places.
See if you can find all three musical notes.

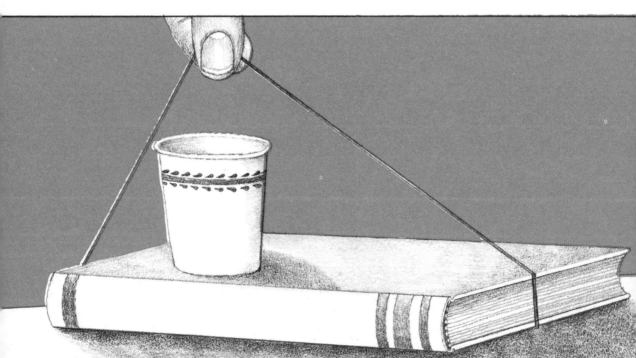

Hear a Heart Beat

Cut the bottom out of a paper cup.
Put the big end on a friend's chest.
Put it right over his heart.
Press your ear against the cup.
Do not touch the cup with your hands.
Listen . . . very quietly.
You will hear his heart beating.
Thump-thump . . . Thump-thump . . . Thump-thump.

This Dog Rolls Over

Partly blow up a long balloon.

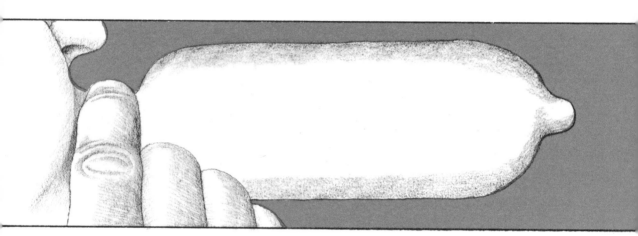

Draw a face and feet on it with a ballpoint pen.

It looks like a funny dog.

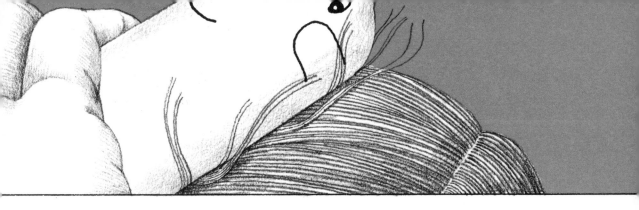

Rub his back hard in your hair.
(Be sure not to rub his stomach.)
Now set him down on the table.
Set him with his stomach down.
Let go.

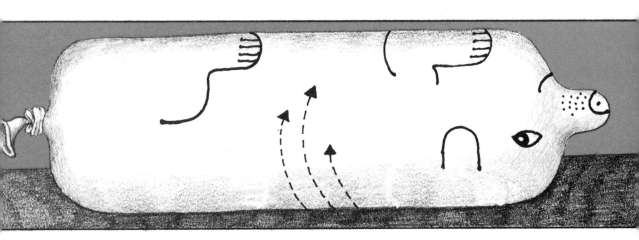

He rolls over on his back!
Static electricity from your hair,
rubbed on the dog's back,
makes his back cling to the table.

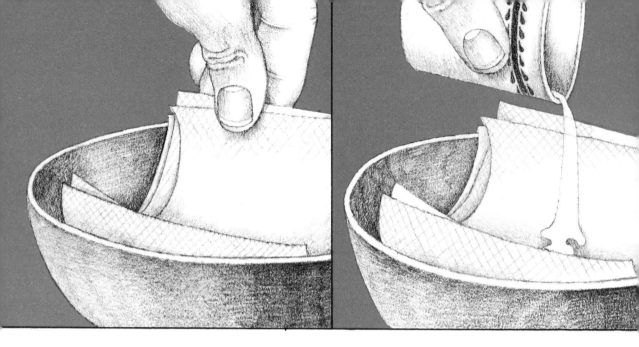

Grow a Snack Garden

Ask your mother if she has some mustard seeds.

Place three paper napkins in a dish.

Wet them with water.

Sprinkle on some mustard seeds.

Wet the napkins every day.

Do not let them dry out.

In a week tiny mustard plants will sprout.

Pick them up.

Eat them.

They are very tasty!

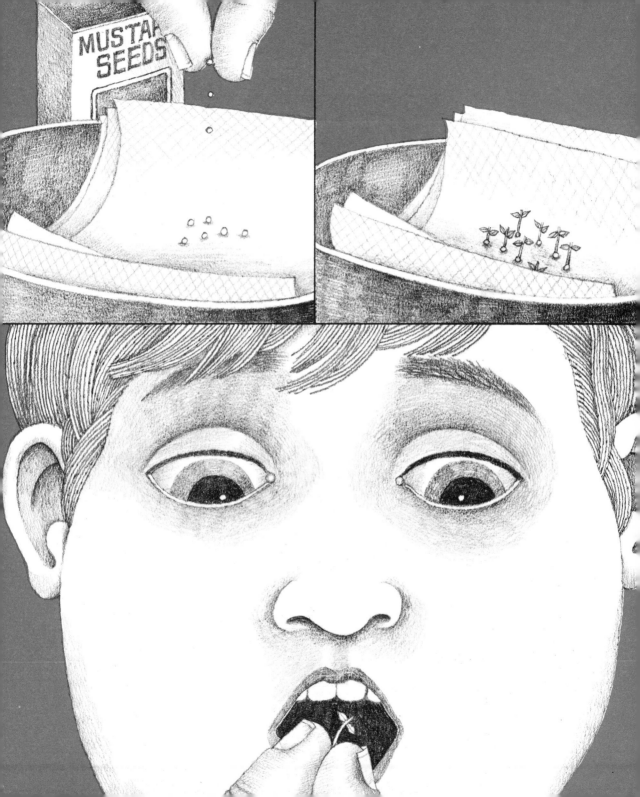

Draw a Glad-Sad Face

Draw this face on a paper plate.
Copy it carefully.
This plate is an optical illusion.
It can fool your eyes.
When you are happy make it glad.
When you are not happy turn it upside down.
Does it look sad?
It fools your eyes when it turns over.

Balancing Curve

Cut a paper plate in half.

Cut the middle out of one half.

Fold the curve in half.

Open it a little.

Now balance the folded curve on a pencil.

Or on your nose.

It looks like it should fall off.

It won't.

It is balanced.

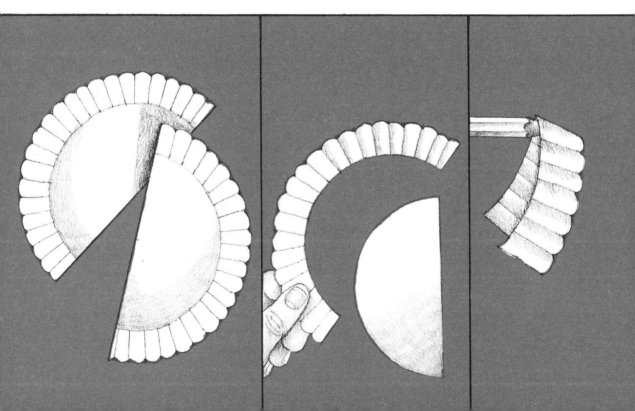

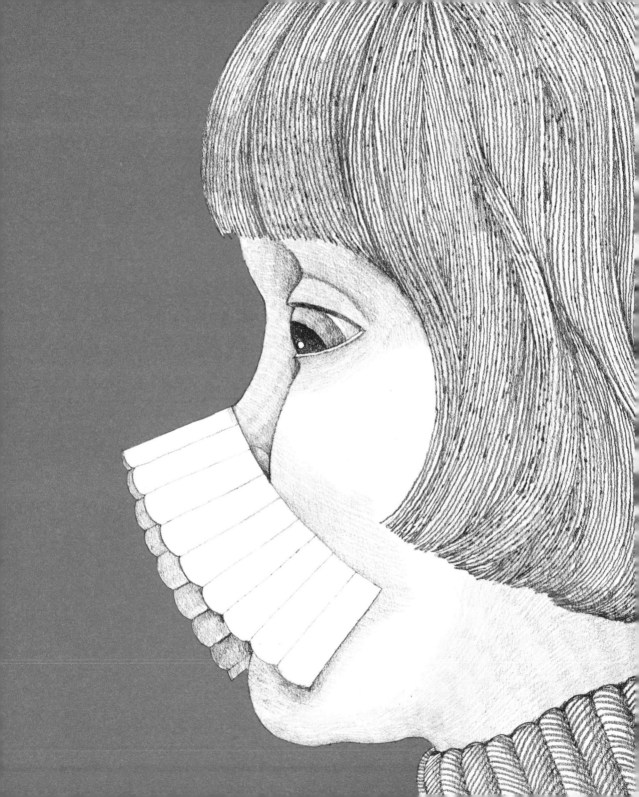

Water Go Round

Push a pencil part way through a paper plate.
Push it right in the middle.
Wiggle the pencil to make the hole loose.
Take it to the sink.
Turn on the water.
Hold one edge of the plate under the water.
You now have a Water Go Round that spins!
How can you make the wheel spin faster?

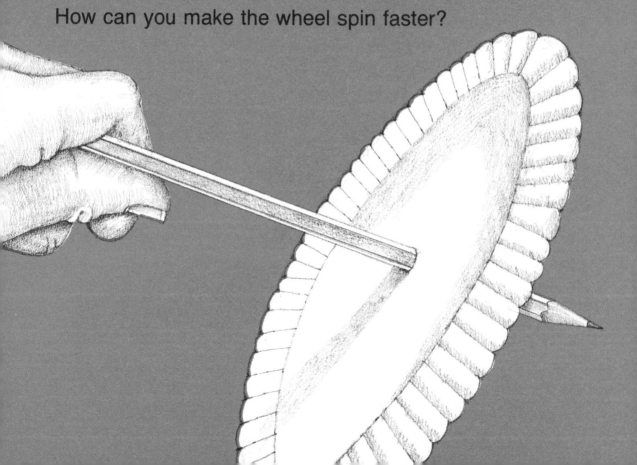

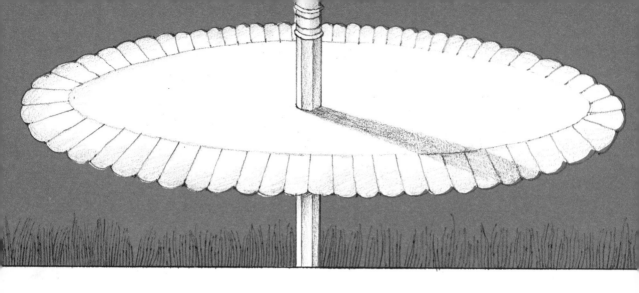

A Shadow Clock

On a bright sunny day
push a pencil half way through a paper plate.
Poke the pencil in the ground.
The pencil makes a shadow on the plate.
Make a mark where it is.

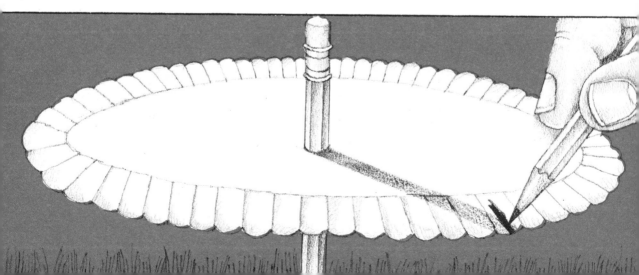

Leave it alone for an hour or more.

When you come back, where is the shadow?

The shadow has moved.

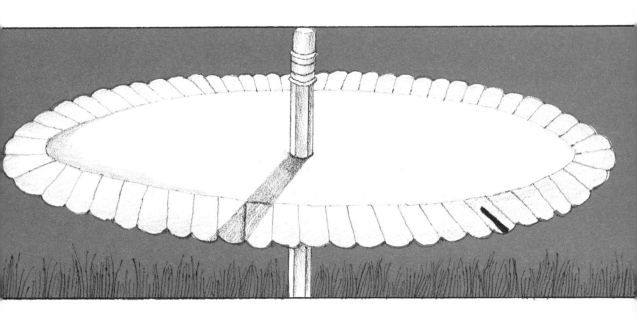

The sun has moved in the sky.

The plate is like a clock with a shadow hand.

People once used sun clocks like this.

The sun helped them measure time.

Wind Spinner

Cut a paper plate from the middle.

Fold the points back and forth.

Wait until the wind is blowing outside.

Set the wind spinner on the sidewalk.

WATCH OUT!

It will zoom away.

The wind can really move things.

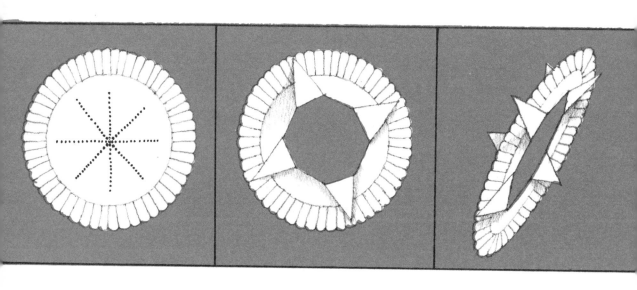

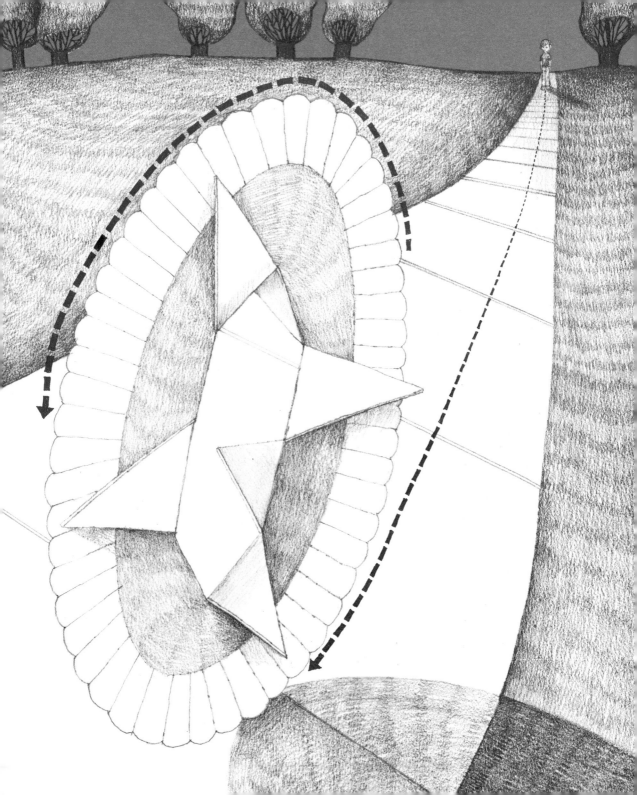

Strange Music From a String

Tie some things on a long string.

Try spoons, pencils, a ruler, and a clothes hanger.

Tie the ends of the string to two chairs.

Place your ear on one end of the string.

Push the string against your ear.

Give a friend a spoon.

Have him tap the things on the string.

Sounds travel through the string.

You hear strange music.

How to Make Raisins Dance

Pour some soda pop in a clear glass.
Drop in some raisins.
They will dance up and down.
Why? Look carefully.
Tiny bubbles stick to them.
The bubbles float the raisins up.
The bubbles disappear at the top.
Then the raisins sink.

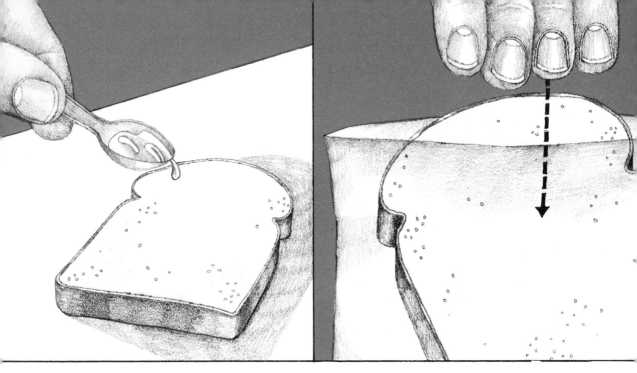

Grow a Mold Garden

Pour a little water on a slice of bread.
Put the bread in a plastic bag.
Blow up the bag.
Close the end with a rubber band.
Let it alone for a week.
Tiny mold plants will grow in the bread.
They are like miniature mushrooms.
And they are very pretty.
(Throw everything away when you are done.
Do not open the bag. It would smell!)

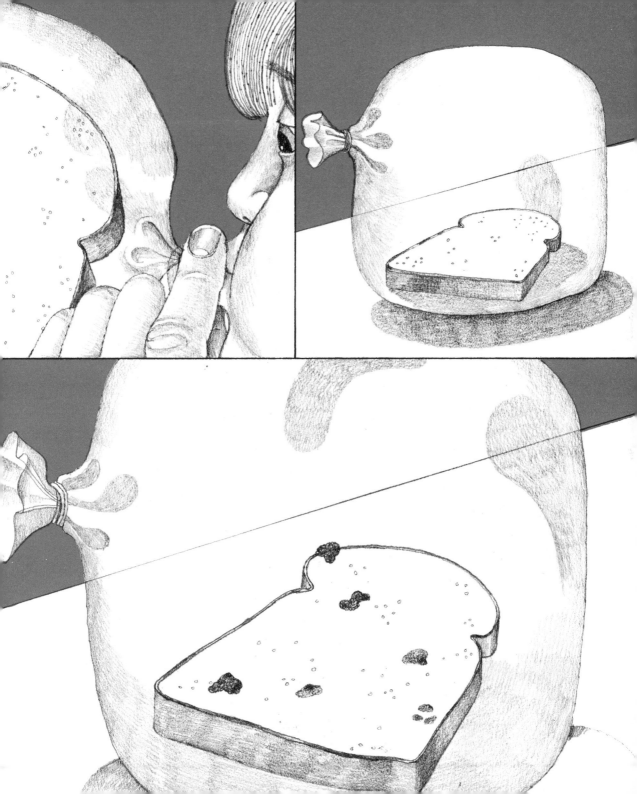

You learned about science
from the toys in this book.
What about other toys?
Can you learn any science from them?
Maybe yes, maybe no.
Play with them.
See if science makes other toys work.

Tricks are to Try

- Make the end of your finger vanish!
- Bounce a real egg on the table!
- Pour water in a pail four feet away!

Are these magic tricks?

Yes? No! They are all science tricks for you.

Science tricks sometimes look like magic . . .

. . . and they are . . .

. . . until you understand how and why they work!

How can you understand them?

By doing them!

. . . . Have fun!

Try a Drinking Straw That Will Not Work

Fill a paper cup with water.

Sip some up with a drinking straw.

Now make a little hole in the straw.

Now try to sip water with it.

You will not be able to.

Air will go in the hole.

You will just get a drink of air.

Have a Drink Upside Down

Have a friend hold you upside down.

Try drinking water from a paper cup.

You have lots of muscles.

Muscles make your body move.

They even help you eat and drink.

Muscles in your throat move water down . . . or up.

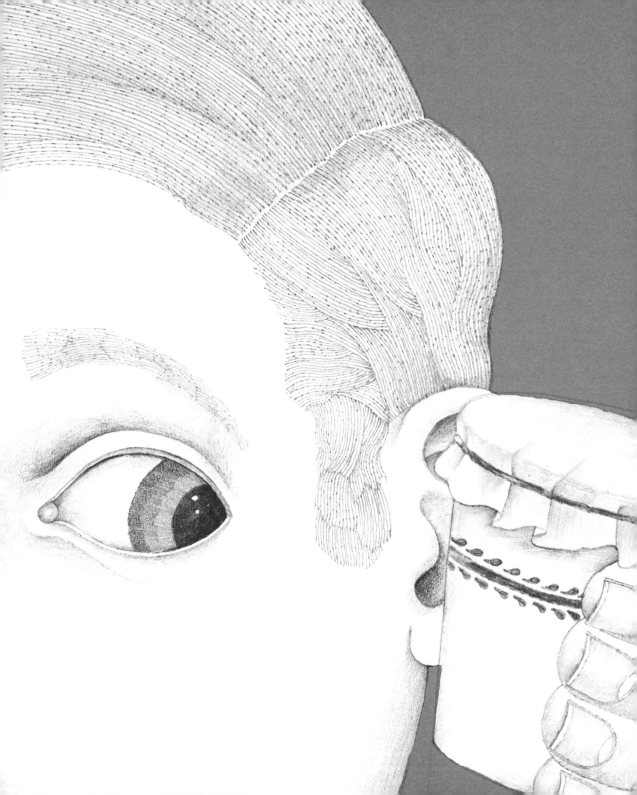

Have You Ever Heard a Fly Walking?

Catch a fly.
Put it in a paper cup.
Cover the cup with paper.
Hold the paper on with a rubber band.
Go where it is very quiet.
Hold the cup against your ear.
The cup is like a drum.
It makes sounds louder.
Stomp, stomp, stomp, stomp.
You will hear the fly walking.

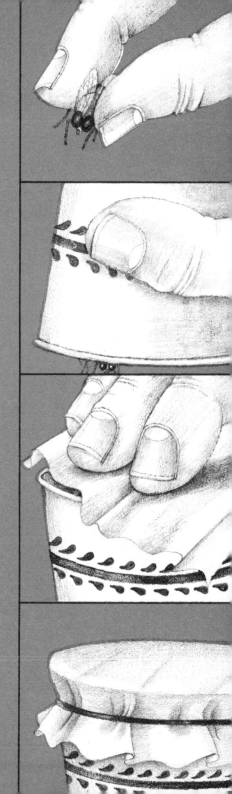

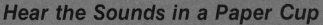

Hear the Sounds in a Paper Cup

There are sounds in a paper cup.
Very tiny sounds.
Hold a cup very close to your ear.
Put your finger in your other ear.
Ask everyone around you to be quiet.
Now listen!
You will hear sounds like wind or ocean waves.
Hold up glasses, pitchers and bottles.
Again in a quiet room . . .
Listen!
They all have sounds in them.
Sounds are everywhere.

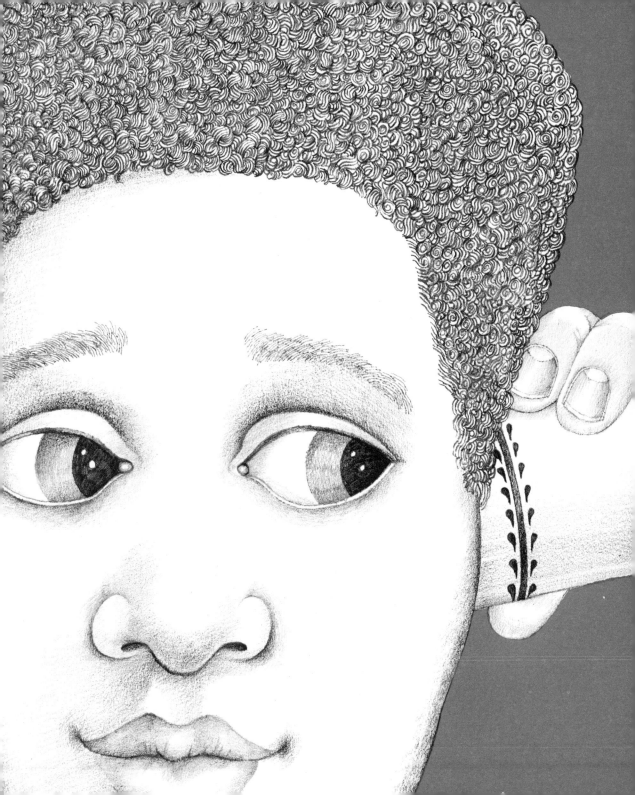

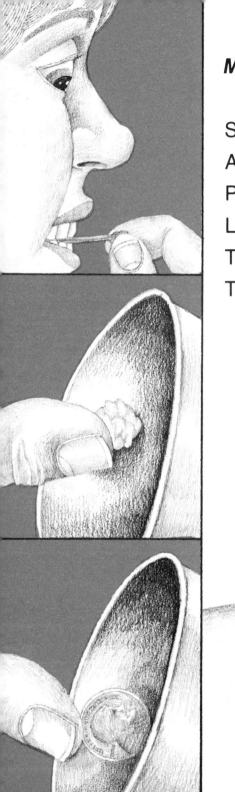

Make a Cup Move by Itself

Stick some chewing gum in a paper cup.
And, stick a coin on the gum.
Put the cup on the table with the coin up.
Let go.
The cup zooms back and forth.
The coin inside makes the cup move.

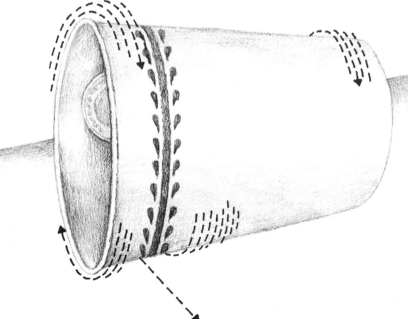

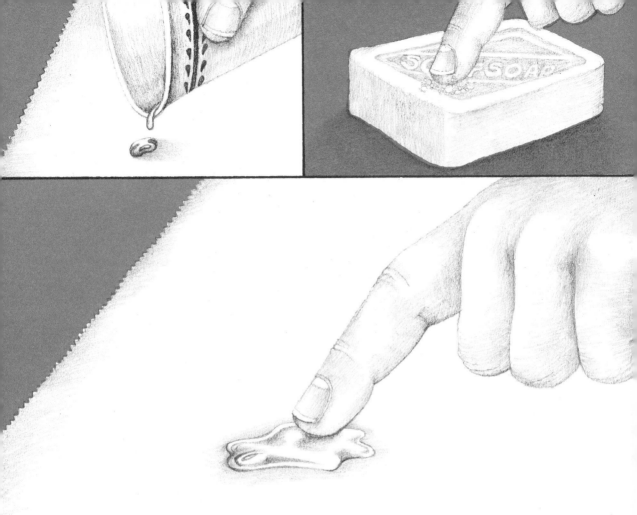

You Can Break a Drop of Water

Pour a big drop of water on a piece of wax paper.

Pour carefully, all in one place.

Rub your finger over a bar of soap.

Touch your soapy finger to the drop of water.

Like magic, soap makes the water drop break.

You stand here . . . .

Pour Water with a Broom

. and pour water in a pail over here.

How? With a broom.

Hold it by the brush end.

Tip it down a little.

Pour water on the handle.

Some water falls off.

Some sticks to the broom and runs down to the pail.

Why? Because water is sticky.

Some water sticks to your hands when you wash.

Some water sticks to your clothes when it rains.

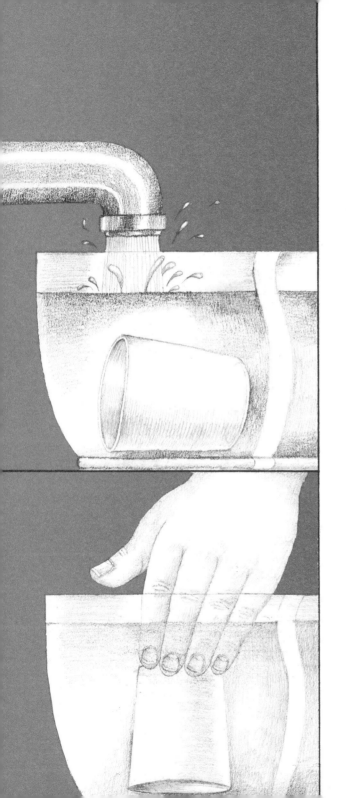

Lift an Upside Down
Glass of Water

Fill a big bowl with water.
Sink a glass in the water.
Reach in and lift the glass.
Lift it upside down.
Keep the open end
under water.
The water will not run out.
Air cannot go into the glass.
Air must go in for the water
to run out.
Lift the glass higher.
Let some air in.
Splash!

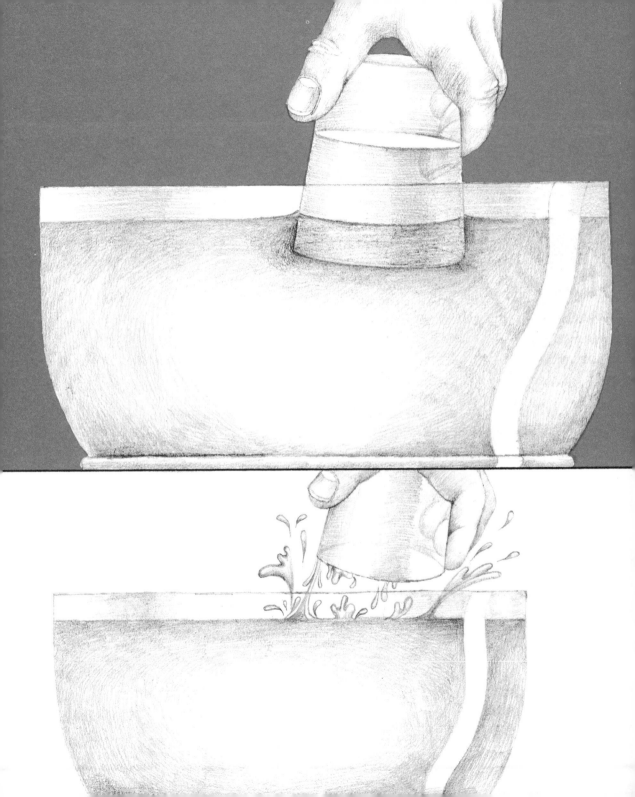

Mix a Glass of Bubbles

Fill a glass half full of water.
Add two big spoonfuls of vinegar.
Stir in a spoonful of dishwashing liquid.
Mix in a big spoonful of baking soda.
Woosh!
The glass is full of bubbles.
Vinegar and baking soda make a gas.
The gas blows tiny bubbles of soap.

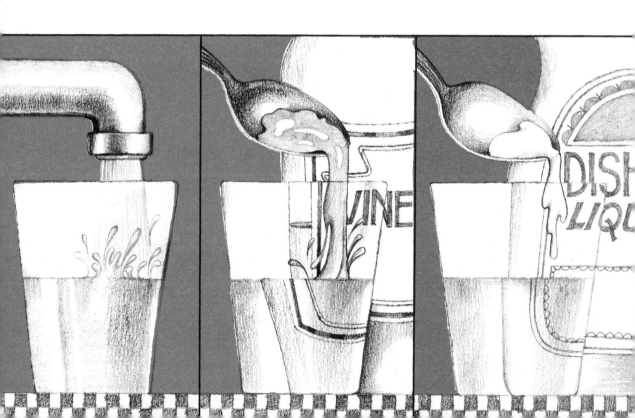

Make an Egg that Bounces

Ask Mom to hard boil an egg for you.

Put it in a drinking glass half full of water.

Then fill the glass with vinegar.

Leave it until tomorrow.

It will look the same.

Feel it.

Bounce it! (Do it gently.)

Vinegar makes the hard shell soft.

Clean a Dirty Penny with Chemicals

Put two spoonfuls of vinegar in a cup.

Sprinkle in some salt. (Five shakes will do.)

Drop in a dirty penny.

Stir it around.

Watch!

See how it shines when you wash it off?

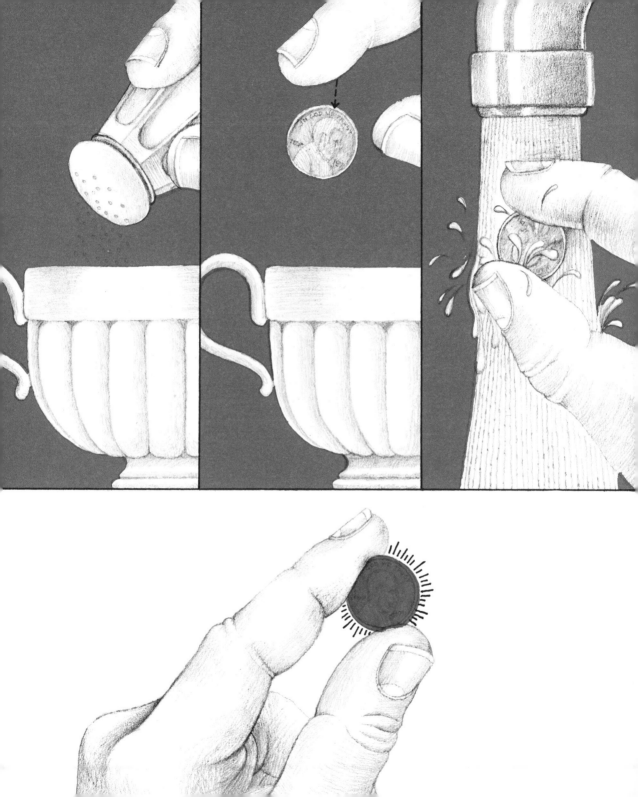

See Water in a Potato

Scoop a hole in a raw potato.
Use a spoon.
Put a spoonful of salt in the hole.
Leave it until tomorrow.
Tomorrow the hole will be full of water.
There is a lot of water in a potato.
Salt makes some of it come out.

An Ice Cube Turns Over by Itself

Put an ice cube in a bowl of warm water.
Do not touch it.
It will turn over all by itself.
Keep watching.
It will turn over again.
And again.
Why?
The warm water melts the bottom of the ice quickly.
The top of the ice gets heavy.
The top falls and the cube turns over.
And over, and over, and over.

Feel How Hot Your Hand Is

Open your hand out flat.
Hold it close to your face.
Leave a little space between your hand and face.
Hold still.
Your body is warm all the time.
Your warm face and hand make the air warm, too.

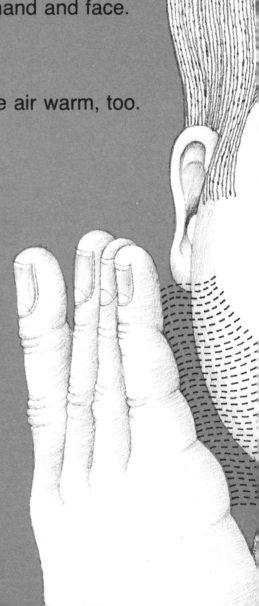

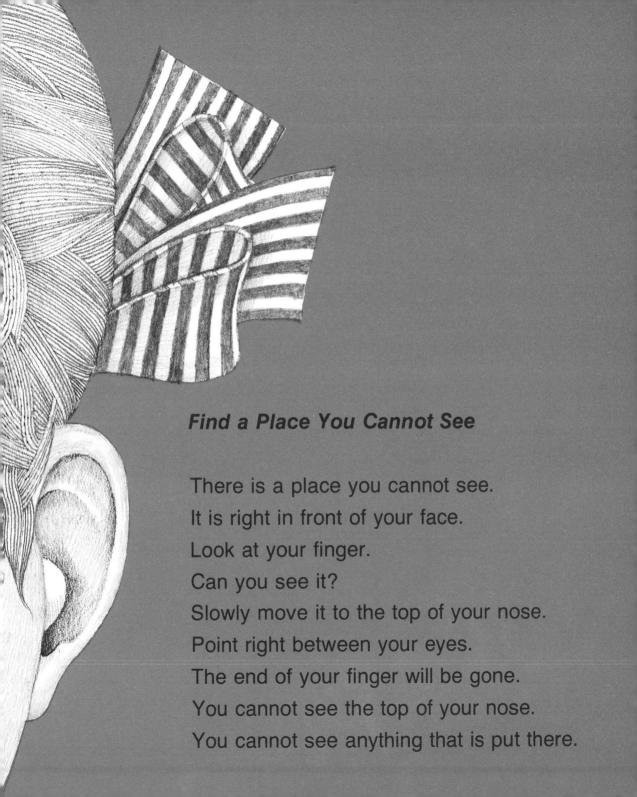

Find a Place You Cannot See

There is a place you cannot see.
It is right in front of your face.
Look at your finger.
Can you see it?
Slowly move it to the top of your nose.
Point right between your eyes.
The end of your finger will be gone.
You cannot see the top of your nose.
You cannot see anything that is put there.

See One Big Eye

You have two eyes.
They both see the same things.
Put your nose on a friend's nose.
Push your faces close together.
What does your friend look like?
Both his eyes look like one.

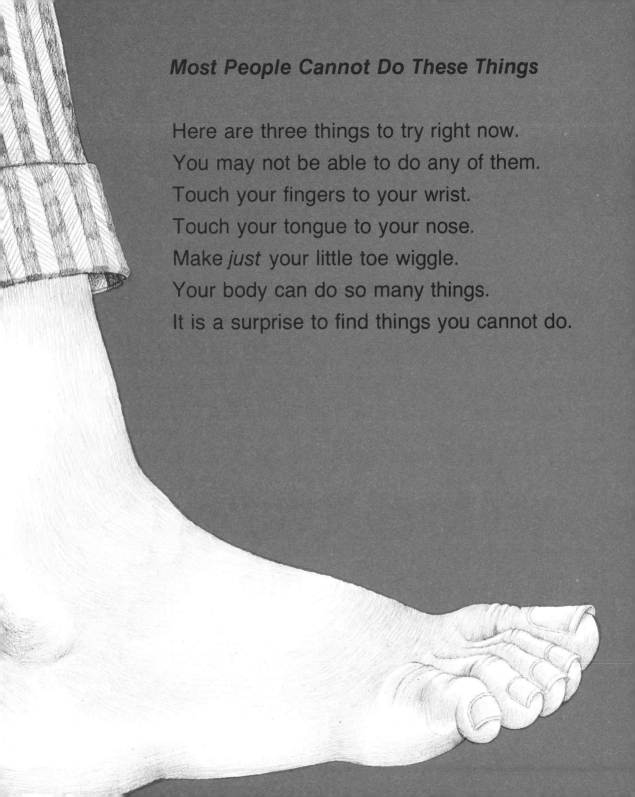

Most People Cannot Do These Things

Here are three things to try right now.
You may not be able to do any of them.
Touch your fingers to your wrist.
Touch your tongue to your nose.
Make *just* your little toe wiggle.
Your body can do so many things.
It is a surprise to find things you cannot do.

Try to Touch Your Toes

Stand with your back up against a wall.
Try to touch your toes, without bending your knees.
You will not be able to do it.
Your body moves forward.
You fall over every time.

Can You Blow This Tent Over?

Cut a piece of paper about this big.
Fold it in half.
Open it like a little tent.
Set it on a table.
Try to blow it over.
You will not be able to do it.
Air holds it on the table.

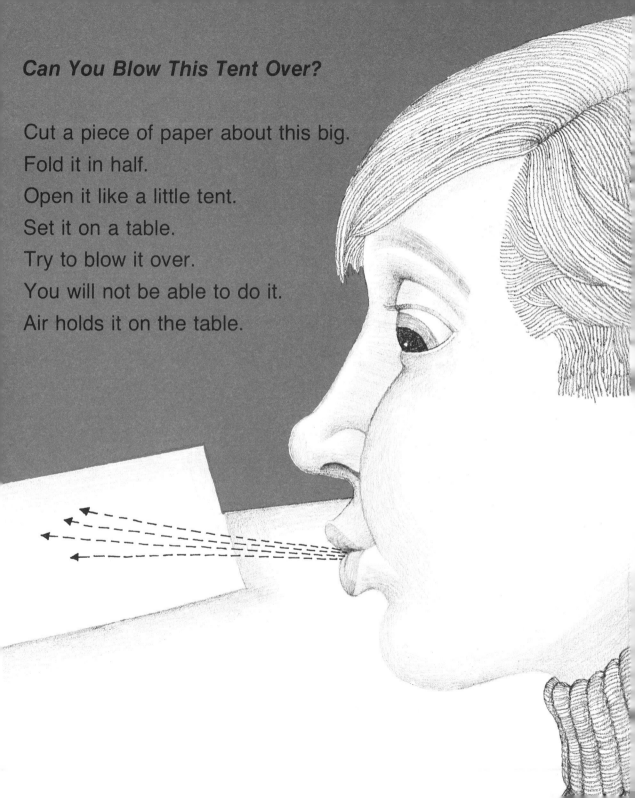

Blow a Piece of Paper Up

Hold a piece of paper by two corners.

Let the end hang down.

Put your lips close to the paper.

Blow hard over the top.

The paper will go up.

Why?

Your breath is like the wind.

The paper is like an airplane wing.

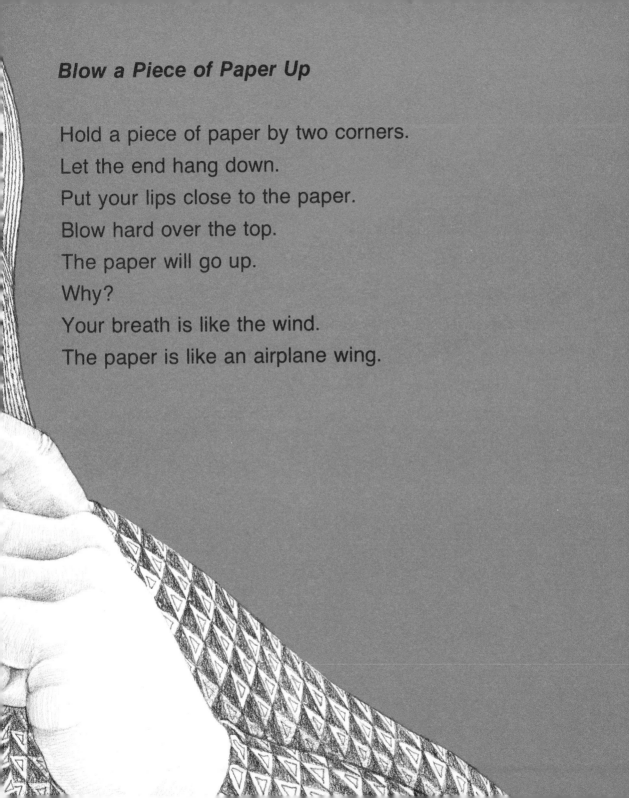

A Sheet of Paper Can Hold Up a Book

Take a sheet of paper.
Then take a book.
Can the paper hold up the book?
Roll the paper into a tube.
Put a rubber band around it.
Set the book on it.
Tubes and pipes are very strong.
They are much stronger than flat things.

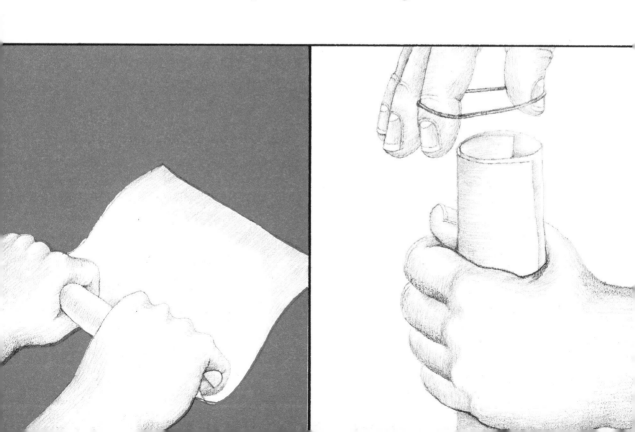

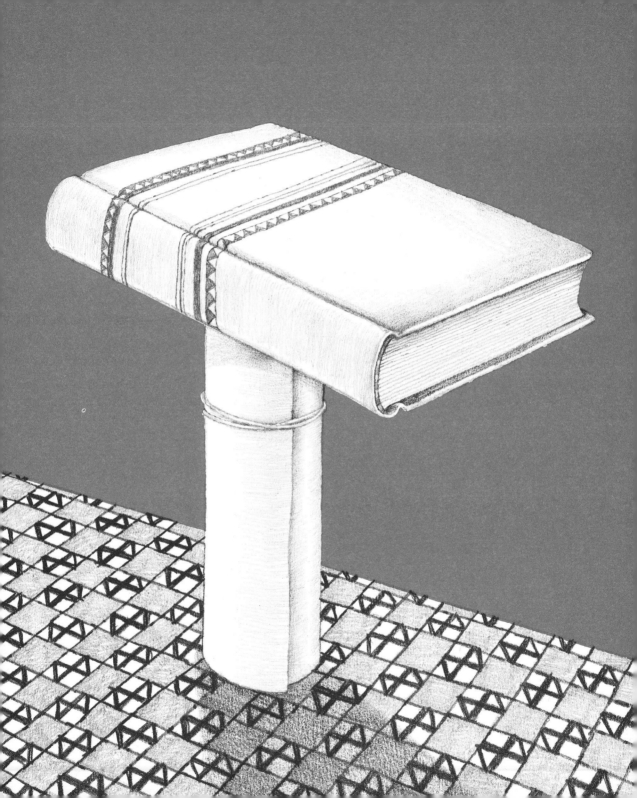

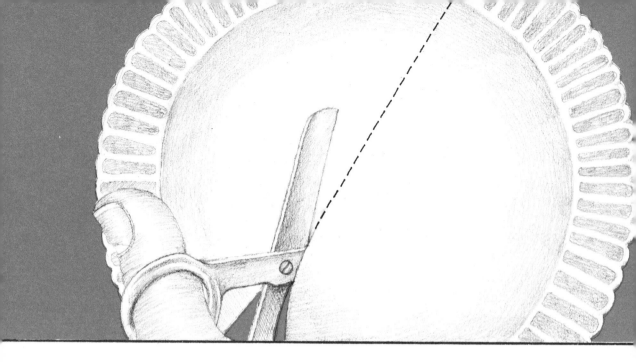

Fool Your Eyes with an Optical Illusion

Cut a paper plate in half.

Cut the middle out of one half.

Cut the curve in half.

Put one piece over the other.

Cut them both the same length.

Hold them side by side.

One looks longer.

But it isn't.

It is an optical illusion.

An optical illusion is a trick that fools your eyes.

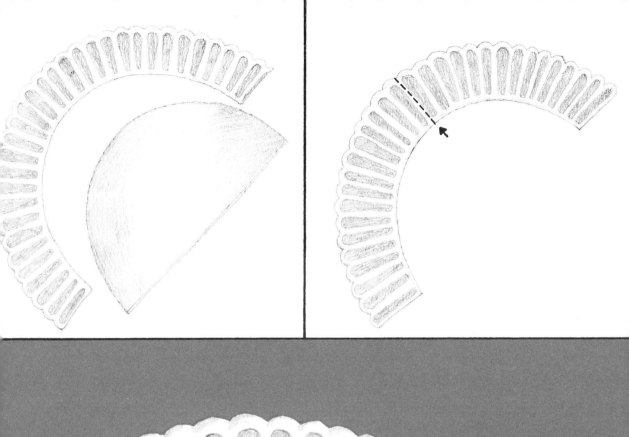

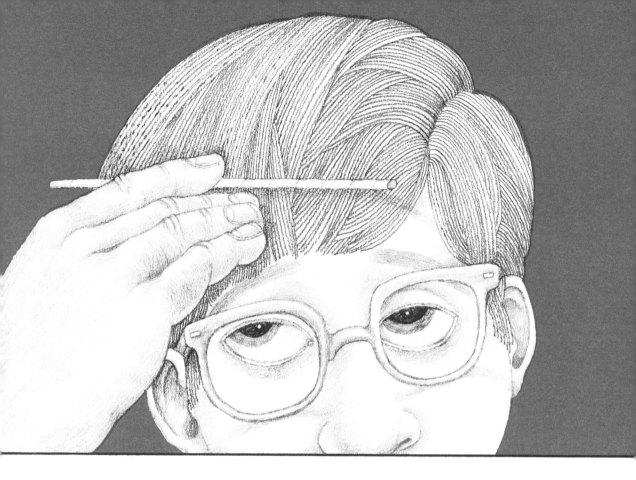

Make a Straw Move with Your Hair

Lay three plastic straws on a table.

Rub another straw in your hair.

Move it near the top straw.

The top straw will roll to it.

Static electricity makes the straw roll.

You made static electricity with your hair.

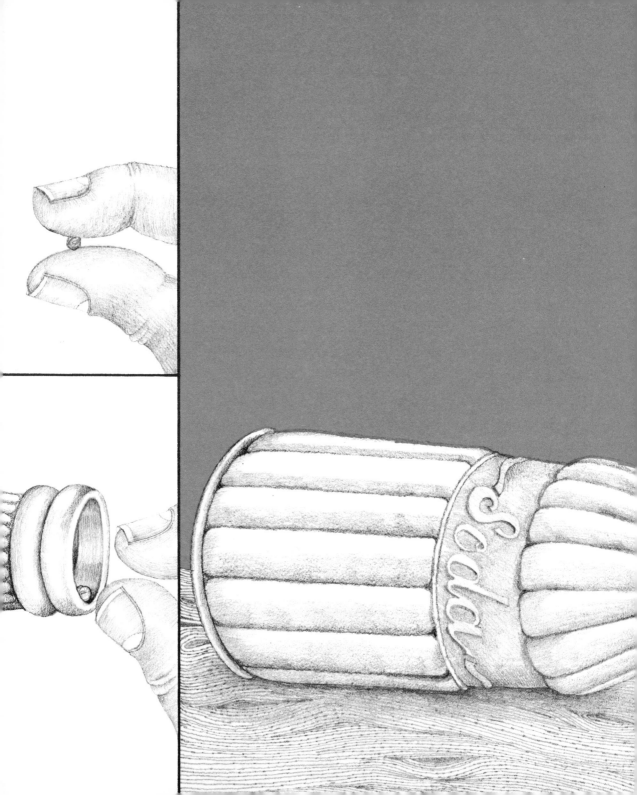

Blow In to Blow a Ball Out

Lay an empty soda bottle on a table.

Roll a little piece of paper into a tiny ball.

Put the ball just inside the bottle.

Try to blow the ball into the bottle.

The ball will pop out.

The bottle is full of air.

The air pushes the ball out.

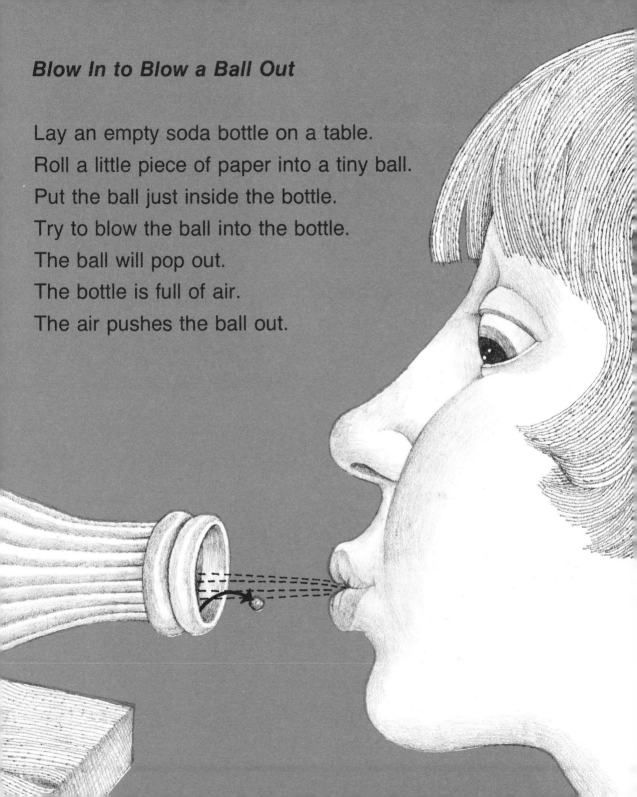

There are no more tricks to try
in this book.
But there are many more
in the world around you.
See how many you can change
from magic into science.